All About
Breeding Cockatiels

Dorothy Bulger

Photography: G. Allen, 17, 24. H.R. Axelrod, 64 bottom. B.D. Lavoy, title page, 4, 6, 12, 16, 20, 25, 28, 29, 30, 32, 33, 36, 37, 40, 41, 44, 45, 48, 49, 52, 53, 56, 57, 60, 61, 64 top, 68, 69, 76, 77, 80, 81, 84, 85. M. Guevara, 8. R. Hanson, 13, 65, 72. Courtesy San Diego Zoo, 21. B. Seed, 92, 93, 96. V. Serbin, 9, 88, 94.

Title page: This two-year-old Normal female, "Bonnie," is of the proper age for breeding. Cockatiels that are less than a year old should not be bred.

Distributed in the UNITED STATES by T.F.H. Publications, Inc., 211 West Sylvania Avenue, Neptune City, NJ 07753; in CANADA by H & L Pet Supplies Inc., 27 Kingston Crescent, Kitchener, Ontario N2B 2T6; Rolf C. Hagen Ltd., 3225 Sartelon Street, Montreal 382 Quebec; in ENGLAND by T.F.H. (Great Britain) Ltd., 11 Ormside Way, Holmethorpe Industrial Estate, Redhill, Surrey RH1 2PX; in AUSTRALIA AND THE SOUTH PACIFIC by Pet Imports Pty. Ltd., Box 149, Brookvale 2100 N.S.W., Australia; in NEW ZEALAND by Ross Haines & Son, Ltd., 18 Monmouth Street, Grey Lynn, Auckland 2 New Zealand; in SINGAPORE AND MALAYSIA by MPH Distributors Pte., 71-77 Stamford Road, Singapore 0617; in the PHILIPPINES by Bio-Research, 5 Lippay Street, San Lorenzo Village, Makati, Rizal; in SOUTH AFRICA by Multipet Pty. Ltd., 30 Turners Avenue, Durban 4001. Published by T.F.H. Publications Inc., Ltd., the British Crown Colony of Hong Kong.

Contents

Preface 5

Breeding Cockatiels 7
  Getting Started 7
  Housing Your Cockatiels 10
  The Nest Box 14
  Sexing Cockatiels 15
  Breeding and Mating 18
  Incubating the Eggs 19
  Infertile Eggs 22
  Normal Hatching 23

Artificial Incubation and Hand-Rearing 31
  Fostering 31
  Artificial Incubation 34
  The Brooder Box 38
  Hand-Rearing 39
  Feeding Techniques 42
  Weaning the Chicks 50

From the Egg to the Cage 55

Hand-Taming and Talking 63
  Hand-Taming 63
  The Talking Cockatiel 70

Grooming and Health Problems 73
  Wing Clipping 73
  Clipping Claws 74
  Trimming the Beak 75
  Possible Problems 75
  The Hospital Cage 87

Helpful Hints 89
  Conclusion 91

Index 94

Cockatiels, like Clyde, are relatively easy birds to keep and to breed; therefore, they are a good choice for beginners.

PREFACE

Cockatiels are one of the most fascinating and interesting birds to breed, train, and enjoy. I am going to tell you exactly how and what my husband, Peter, and I did to raise our cockatiels from the egg to the cage. It is quite a rewarding experience to watch an ugly little chick become a beautiful bird within just a few weeks. I will tell you of our successes and of our failures.

We are very lucky to have a friend such as our veterinarian, William J. Taylor, D.V.M. When I told him that I wanted to write this book and asked if he would consider acting as my medical consultant, he quickly agreed. When learning about birds, you will find that there are always questions to be asked and answers to be sought. Dr. Taylor was very gracious when I handed him a list of questions. Not only did he answer my many inquiries, but he also took the time to explain in detail the reason for the different methods being used. Now that this book is completed, I am sure that he is overjoyed, as my telephone calls to him are not as frequent or as frantic.

It is said that a picture is worth a thousand words. Thanks to Bruce D. Lavoy's photography, I have some outstanding and unusual pictures to share with you. Bruce did a great job, and I can't thank him enough.

Of course I must thank our producing cockatiels, Bonnie and Clyde. Without their appreciation of the nesting box, none of this would be possible.

Comparison of a seven-day-old nestling with a five-week-old fledgling. The egg tooth is still partially visible on the younger bird.

BREEDING COCKATIELS

Breeding cockatiels at home is a rewarding experience that you will probably never forget. The cockatiel thrives on love and attention from its human family. It is not just a one-person bird; it will be devoted to each member of the family and look forward to being the center of attraction.

Training the cockatiel is easily done when you use patience and love and reward it with a favorite treat. You will enjoy watching its antics as it plays in its cage—ringing bells, climbing ladders, taking baths, admiring itself in the mirror, singing songs, whistling, and just having a good time.

Caring for it is easy, as it is one of the smaller birds. It doesn't take up much space, and is a clean little bird.

The cockatiel is native to Australia. It measures about 12 in. from the crest to the end of its long tail feathers. Its normal life span is between ten and fourteen years.

GETTING STARTED

The hardest part of any project is the beginning. We know what we want to accomplish, but how do we get started?

The first question you must ask yourself is whether you want a young cockatiel that you can hand-tame yourself, or an older one that is ready for breeding. A young bird can easily be found in your local pet shop. If you want an older bird, you may have better luck locating one through your

House your cockatiel in a roomy cage designed with horizontal wires that will facilitate climbing.

Opposite:
Exercise great care whenever you let your pet out of its cage. Untamed birds, in particular, may be difficult to retrieve from a high perch such as a curtain rod.

local newspaper advertisements; a large percentage of these birds are sold with their cages and accessories.

If you buy a "secondhand" bird, be sure to check it out thoroughly, as you don't want to buy someone else's troubles. I have turned down many birds because they have had loose droppings, puffy eyes, or runny noses, or just because I had a bad feeling about them. Once I turned down a bird because the owner assured me that it was finger-tamed; however, it would only get on his finger if no one else was in the room. Needless to say, you can't believe everything you are told. Never be afraid to bring with you someone who knows what to look for. If you have no one to go shopping with you and you think there might be something wrong with the bird, don't buy it, as you may not get a health guarantee. If you are hesitant about buying from a private source, your pet shop may part with a pair of their breeders, for a price. You will get a "health" guarantee from many pet shops, but you'll almost never get one from a private seller—which is of course one good reason why it pays to deal with pet shops in the first place.

Each pet shop has its own policy on returning birds. I have found that many of them will not give a cash refund but will exchange the bird for another one. Whenever buying from a pet shop, be sure that you know what their policy is and exactly what their guarantee covers.

HOUSING YOUR COCKATIELS

I can't suggest strongly enough that you make sure you have enough room for your cockatiels, as having a true pair means there will be more to come if you supply them with a nest box. Even without a nest box, some cockatiels have been known to lay eggs on the bottom of the cage, although this is not likely to happen very often. After breeding our first pair of cockatiels, we bought more pairs. One thing led to another, and now our dining room is a bird room.

Our breeding cage is 21 in. square and 24 in. high, with a nest box 9½ in. wide, 11½ in. deep, and 11½ in. tall attached to the back. We cut only enough bars from the cage to allow the cockatiels to enter the 2½ in. hole in the nest box.

Be sure that you save the bars that were cut from the cage, as you can have them replaced when the nest box is not needed. If you bring the cage to an automobile repair shop, the mechanic can replace the bars by brazing them back to the cage. When you get the cage back home, spray the repair with a nontoxic paint, and the cage will be back to normal.

Cages come equipped with two perches as well as water and seed containers. Cuttlebone and a mineral block can be placed near one perch; water, with vitamins added, and a supply of grit, cockatiel seed mix, and Petamine (a high-protein food) near the other one. The bottom of the cage should be lined with newspaper cut to size, with an adequate quantity of grit sprinkled over it. Cockatiels like to peck and scratch on the bottom. You may want to put another dish in the cage for their treats, such as leafy greens, carrots, pieces of apple and so on.

The floor of the nest box should be covered with a small amount of coarse sawdust to absorb the droppings of the chicks.

The cage should be situated so that the nest box is close to a wall. This arrangement will prevent anyone from walking around or near the nest box and alarming the soon-to-be-parents. Be sure that the cage is not placed near a window or a door, as a draft will cause colds and possibly death.

Remember, cleanliness is one of the most important rules to follow to ensure having healthy birds. Be sure to change the water and food and to clean the bottom of the cage daily. Once a week the cage, as well as the perches, should be given a good scrubbing. Everything must be completely dry before the cockatiels are returned to the cage. This is

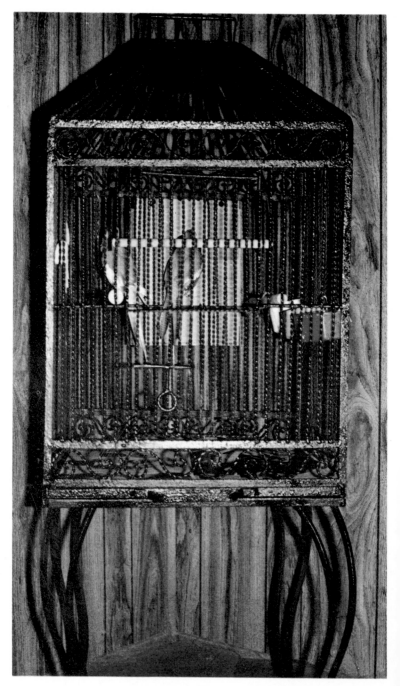

Be certain to select a cage that is appropriate for cockatiels, one that is sturdy enough to withstand the cockatiel's chewing urges and one that offers plenty of room for movement (opposite). Since it is recommended that the cage floor be cleaned daily, it makes sense to purchase a cage with a removable bottom (above).

13

when a second pair of perches comes in handy as you can use one pair each week, allowing the other to dry thoroughly. If set out in the sun, the perches will dry within a few hours. Tree branches make better perches than do standard dowels. The branches with their different diameters exercise the bird's feet and toes, and they have the added feature of bark for the cockatiels to chew on.

Cockatiels are very playful and inquisitive birds. There are a variety of toys on the market to keep your pets amused. They especially like mirrors (the metal kind), bells, wooden blocks, and hanging rings.

THE NEST BOX

Nest boxes can be homemade or purchased from the pet store. If you are making your own nest box, be sure that all of the joints are tight. If the joints have gaps, a multitude of problems can occur. Loose joints permit drafts and dampness to enter, which will quickly kill the newly hatched chicks. Another problem will arise when the chicks are roaming around in the box. They could very easily lose a toe if they should stumble over a gap. A tightly constructed box will hold the much-needed heat the parents supply for their young.

The use of screws instead of nails when assembling the nest box will ensure tight-fitting joints; nails do not secure the wood so well as screws do. If the box needs to be disassembled for any reason, removing them is simple, and the wood will not split.

Directly under the entrance hole there should be a dowel perch for the parent birds to stand on. The dowel should protrude 2½ to 3 in. into the cage, and the same amount into the nest box. Without a perch on the box, the parents could injure the chicks by landing on them. The perch allows the parents to view the chicks and also to keep an eye on the cage from inside the box.

Before being attached to the cage, the nest box must be thoroughly cleaned. If you scrub it with hot water, set it out in the sun until it is completely dry. A good mite spray is beneficial. If there are any mites in the box, or if you just want to feel safe, spray the box, let it dry, then scrub it with a mild soap and hot water. You may not see any mites in the box, as they are very tiny and live in the cracks of the wood, but it is better to be safe than sorry.

In the wild, cockatiels lay their eggs in a cavity of a tree. Trying to create a natural breeding spot for the cockatiel in your home is almost impossible. You would have to find a hollowed out log free from insects and be able to have an inspection door for you to check on the chicks. The commercial nest box has proven to be the next best thing to nature. In captivity cockatiels readily accept the nest box.

SEXING COCKATIELS

Sexing cockatiels (before their first molt) is extremely difficult, but distinguishing a young bird from an adult bird is easily done. The younger bird will have a tighter beak, pinker feet, and softer feathers.

The adult gray cockatiel is very easily sexed. The female will have a gray head and body, and the male has a yellow head with a gray body.

Other color varieties are much harder to sex. To sex the young bird, some breeders will pull a single flight feather and the outer left tail feather. When the new feathers grow in, the female will have light colored stripes on the tail feather and spots on the wing feather. The male's new feathers will be a solid color. This sex test is not always accurate in pied cockatiels as they frequently lack black pigment in the tail and primary feathers, as do the lutinos.

Holding the bird and placing your finger over the vent and feeling the pelvic bones is another way to sex the cockatiel. The female's bones are wider apart and have more flexibility than the male's. The difference is slight, but the

Before mating can take place, it must be established that one has a true pair (a male and a female). Sexing is best accomplished after a bird's first molt.

Opposite:
When the hen is ready to mate, she crouches low on the perch and raises her tail feathers. The cock then mounts her (above) and as their vents meet, copulation takes place (below).

17

more experienced breeder and your veterinarian can quickly sex the bird using this method.

A very unscientific method of sexing is to place cockatiels in front of a mirror. The male is quite taken with himself and will whistle and sing to his image for long periods of time, while the female is very easily distracted. This is not a tried and true method as some females are just as vain as a male.

Both males and females will hiss when they are upset, although the female seems to hiss more frequently and is the quickest to bite. Once again, this is not an accurate sex test.

BREEDING AND MATING

Now that we have our cage and the nest box ready, our pair of cockatiels can move into their new home. It is best that the birds be at least a year old. They can breed when they're younger, but younger parents often prove to be incompetent.

Don't be alarmed if the cockatiels seem to avoid the nest box at first. Eventually the male will inspect it thoroughly. Within a few days, he will encourage the female to enter the box and set up housekeeping. You will notice that as each day goes by she is spending more time in the box. Breeding behavior begins.

You will enjoy the antics of courtship. There will be a lot of cooing, kissing, snuggling, grooming and feeding each other. They will cuddle close, sing to each other and just enjoy being together. As they get used to your being around, they will not hesitate to court in front of you. They will have their little squabbles, but they will always end up preening each other, and the pair-bonding continues.

When the hen is ready for mating she lowers her back, giving a flat appearance. While singing his favorite song, the male will mount and stand on her back, swinging his tail to the side and under her until their vents meet.

Now is the time for you to place a bowl of room-temperature water in the cage. The hen will sit in the water from time to time to keep the egg inside her moist. If the egg is allowed to dry, the hen will become egg-bound. Egg binding occurs when the egg is stuck in the oviduct and cannot pass. If the hen has the bowl of water to use at her convenience and there are no other problems, she should not get egg bound. If the hen does become egg bound, she will sit in a huddled position and become very irritable. An egg-bound hen cannot live more than a day or so in this condition. There is no medication that can be administered orally to prevent egg binding because it cannot get into the oviduct to lubricate the egg. The best treatment is heat and moisture. Holding the hen over warm steam will usually loosen the egg so that it can pass.

Some breeders will pull the tail feathers from the female to allow the male easy access to her vent. This writer doesn't believe that this is necessary but believes instead that nature will take its course.

During copulation, the male will sing and chatter until his dismount, which is within ten minutes. Copulation occurs several times a day until a full clutch of eggs (usually five) is laid. The eggs are laid approximately every other day.

INCUBATING THE EGGS

Do not be alarmed if the hen seems to ignore the eggs the first few days; she will sit on them when there are two or three. Both parents will take the responsibility of sitting on the eggs. They may even separate the eggs into two groups so they can sit together in the box. The incubation period of the eggs is usually eighteen days, each one hatching in the order that it was laid. If the hen didn't sit on the first one or two in the beginning, these may hatch almost together. The rest should hatch every other day.

The parents will not soil the nest box. They will control

Cockatiel chicks are born with a covering of soft, yellow down. Within only a few days, feather development begins and will continue for several weeks.

Opposite:
Both parents share the responsibility to incubate the eggs. Here both have come out of the nest box for food and exercise (above). A reconstructed egg that hatched in only ten minutes, although some take hours to hatch (below).

themselves until they come out into the cage. Their droppings are softer and runnier than usual. The color is a lighter shade of green with quite a bit of white. You will notice that both parents are working on the cuttlebone more than usual. Be sure that you have extra cuttlebones on hand.

Do not "sneak up" to the nest box, as this could alarm the parents. If they get frightened, they will flutter around in the box, possibly causing the eggs to roll into each other and crack or even break. When approaching the cage, make your presence known by talking, singing, or whistling. Tap gently on the nest box. This action will encourage the birds to leave the box, letting you inspect the condition of the eggs.

It is good practice to check the eggs daily, making sure there aren't any broken ones. If there is one there, remove it immediately. If it is stuck to the bottom of the box, use a piece of warm, wet cotton to remove it. Make absolutely sure that you completely dry the box and any other egg you may have touched. Do not let the parents peck at or eat the broken egg. Some breeders believe that if a bird gets a taste of egg, it can never be trusted again. Keep an eye on the rest of the eggs. If there is another broken egg, you may want to incubate the rest of them artificially. If there is only one broken egg, let the parents finish the incubation.

Do not try to wash the cage during the incubation period. You will be able to change the food and water and clean the bottom of the cage daily. A complete scrub-down of the cage will frighten the parents. You will be able to remove the perches for cleaning. Once again, I can't stress enough that the perches be perfectly dry before returning them to the cage.

INFERTILE EGGS

A week after the eggs have been laid, you can check their fertility by holding them up to a strong light. A penlight works well, as you will be able to put the light right to the egg and not have any light shining in your eyes. A fertile egg will appear to be half full. Each egg you check must be at least seven days old. Since one cannot be sure which egg was laid first, it is best to check for fertility seven days from when the last egg was laid. If you do "candle" the eggs, remember that the first egg laid may have hatched before the last egg appears fertile.

There are many causes of infertile eggs. One of the most common causes with caged birds is improper diet. Improper handling of the eggs can also cause infertility. If you must handle the egg, be aware of how thin and fragile the shell is. It absorbs the moisture and body heat from your hand. As the egg develops, handling it is less dangerous. Incomplete copulation (when the vents have had poor contact) can also cause infertility.

NORMAL HATCHING

The eggs will hatch in the order in which they were laid, a new chick every other day. Do not open the nest box to peek for a few hours as the chicks are wet and need time to dry. The newborn chick is covered with wet down which will fluff up when it is dry. Opening the box while the chick is wet will create a draft, giving the chick a chill. A chill will quickly kill a newborn chick.

When the chick is dry and the parents are out in the cage feeding, carefully reach into the nest box and remove the broken shell. More than once a newborn chick has accidentally fallen into a broken shell and smothered to death. Never reach into the box if the parents are in it. If the parents are in the box and fail to push the shell away from the chick, tap on the outside of the box to get the parents' attention. They will come out to investigate. Carefully open the inspection door of the nest box and remove the broken shell.

Parent birds store ingested food in the part of their esophagus known as the crop. This stored food is then regurgitated and fed to the chicks (above and below).

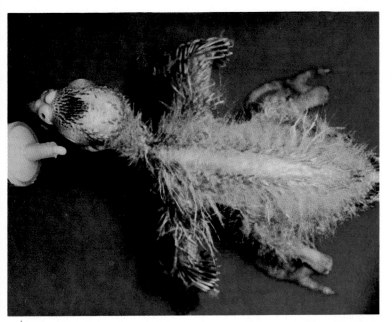

Feather growth is apparent everywhere on this seven-day-old chick but on the back of its head and along the spine (above). These two chicks are also seven days old, although they are seventeen hours apart in age (below).

Be sure that there is ample food in the cage, as the parents will be eating constantly. They will be feeding the chicks by regurgitating partially digested food into their tiny little mouths. Both parents will feed the chicks. The parents do not feed the chicks as soon as they are hatched; they wait for as long as eleven or twelve hours. If they wait any longer, the chicks will very quickly dehydrate and die.

The chicks must be watched carefully for the first few days. Sometimes the parent will spill some of the regurgitated food on the chick's back, eat it again, then continue to feed the chick. After the feeding, the parent will try to clean up the chick. The food is very sticky, and the parent could accidentally hurt, or even kill, the chick. You should take the chick from the box and inspect it for any spillage. If it is soiled, carefully clean it with a piece of cotton and warm water. If there is any food left on the beak, it will become hard and crusty. Remove it carefully, as the beak is still soft. Dry the chick completely and return it to the box.

Whenever you have to remove any of the baby chicks from the nest box, be sure to keep them warm. If you have to keep the chick out longer than just a few minutes, try holding it in a soft hand towel, which is very hard to do if you are trying to wash and dry it. A temperature change of ± 5 F. is acceptable, as the temperature fluctuates about that much when the parents leave the nest box to feed and get exercise.

When the chicks are about five weeks old, they will begin to leave the nest box. Sprinkle food and grit on the bottom of the cage. They will learn from watching the parents how to break open and eat the seed. When you are absolutely sure that the chicks are eating totally on their own, you can put them into a separate cage.

Sprinkle food and grit on the bottom of the chicks' new cage until you are sure that they know how to eat from the food cups. Put a sturdy water dish, one that can't be tipped over, on the floor. Make sure that the water dish is not large enough for the chicks to walk through. Letting the chicks have wet feet is a sure invitation for a cold. The water may have to be changed three or four times a day as the chicks will drop their seeds into it. Vitamins should be added to the water at each changing.

If a perch is located close to the bottom of the cage, it will be easier and safer for the chicks to learn how to stand on it. Place the chick on the perch. It will fall off quickly. Work with each chick for about twenty minutes at a time, perch-training it. Within a day or two, they will be stepping up on the perch by themselves.

After a week or so, place another perch at the middle of the cage. If you put a ladder (your pet store has many different sizes) between the middle of the cage to the floor, the chick will learn quickly to use the higher perch. At this time, raise the feed cups. Within another week you will be able to remove the bottom perch as the chick will lose all interest in it.

This four-week-old bird shows off its newly feathered wing. In a few days, it will begin to leave the nest box and become independent of its parents.

Opposite:
At five weeks of age, the chick can be separated from its parents and placed in a cage of its own, complete with perches, toys, food, a cuttlebone, and water (above). This chick has learned to balance itself on the lower perch which has been placed near the food and water dishes (below).

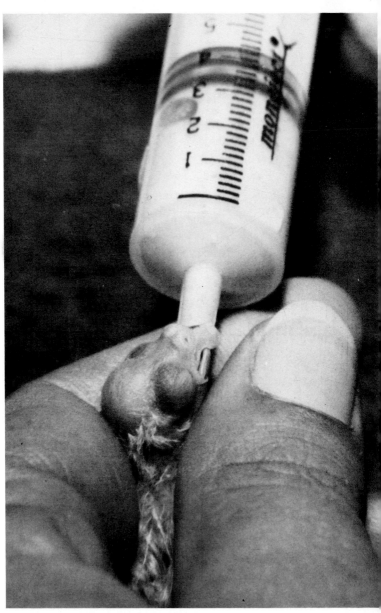

Hand-reared chicks should be fed every two to three hours for the first few days. Do not be alarmed if the young cockatiel that you are feeding suddenly bobs its head up and down; this is instinctive behavior. Just hold the chick firmly, but gently, to ensure the formula is being swallowed.

ARTIFICIAL INCUBATION AND HAND-REARING

If the parents neglect or kill the first one or two chicks, not all is lost. You have two choices for saving the rest of the clutch.

FOSTERING

The first choice is to find foster parents. If you don't know anyone who happens to have a pair of cockatiels sitting on a clutch of eggs, call your local pet shop or your veterinarian. They may know of someone who does. You can offer one of the chicks as "payment" for the incubation and rearing of your clutch. Anyone who is breeding cockatiels will know what you are going through and will probably be more than willing to help you out at your time of desperate need.

I used foster parents once, recommended by my veterinarian, and found it to work quite well. To transport the eggs, you must be extremely careful to keep the eggs warm. Put a few layers of cotton in the bottom of a small box and place the eggs in the box. Next, wrap the box in a heavy towel to protect the inside of the box from any drafts or allowing the heat to escape. I brought my eggs to the veterinarian's office, and he in turn gave them to the owner of the foster parents.

Sometimes parent birds are unable to incubate and rear their young. Here is where an incubator comes in handy. This styrofoam model has a water reservoir in the bottom to keep the eggs moist and a heating element attached to the inside of the top to keep the eggs warm (opposite). Newborn chicks emerge wet from their shell, but in a few hours the matted down begins to dry (above). A few hours after hatching, the chicks receive their first meal. After each feeding, the crop will bulge as it fills with food (below).

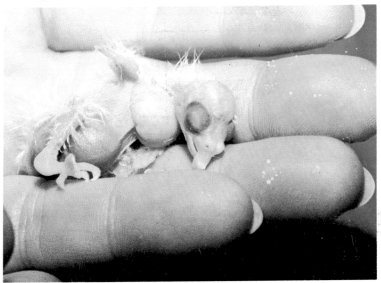

The foster parents readily accepted my eggs, and hatched them without any problems. I did, however, have to take the chicks back from the foster parents when they were three weeks old because they started to feather-pluck the babies. We can only assume that the parents wanted their nest empty so they could breed again. Within a week the hen was laying more eggs. Taking the chicks at three weeks old, I had to hand-rear them for another three weeks. The chicks grew to be healthy, beautiful cockatiels, and the cost to me was one of the chicks.

ARTIFICIAL INCUBATION

The other alternative is to purchase an incubator. We purchased an inexpensive styrofoam incubator at a pet shop. You may have to shop around for one, as not all pet shops carry incubators. If you are lucky enough to have time to wait, the pet shop personnel will be able to order one for you.

Set the temperature of the unit at 100 F. (38 C.) and let it run for at least eight hours, checking the temperature hourly and readjusting the control if needed. When the temperature stops fluctuating and stays at 100 F. for a few hours, the incubator is ready for use. Before placing the eggs into the incubator, add warm water to the bottom of the unit if it is made with a water reservoir; if it is not, you will have to lightly spray the eggs as you are turning them.

If you want all of the eggs to hatch together instead of every other day, you can store them in a cool place where the temperature is between 40 F. and 60 F. until the complete clutch has been laid. The eggs must be turned completely once each day during this storage period. Having the eggs hatch at the same time makes it easier for you to care for them. There will be no need for you to have different formulas or feeding times, as the chicks all will be on the same schedule. It can be quite a hassle if the chicks are of different ages and are on different formulas with different feeding schedules. When the time comes for weaning the chicks, it will be easier to wean them all together, instead of one at a time.

With a pencil or a felt-tip marker, mark an "X" on each egg. Do not use a ball-point pen, for it may puncture the fragile, thin egg. During the incubation period, the eggs must be turned at least three times a day. Every other time you turn the eggs, the "X" will be on the top of the eggs. On a daily basis, be sure to check the water level in the incubator, as the constant heat will cause it to evaporate quickly.

If your incubator doesn't have a water reservoir, you will have to spray the eggs lightly—not soaking them—with warm water each time you turn them. If the eggs are not kept moist, the chicks will be weakened and therefore cannot break their way out of the shell and will die. When the parents are incubating the eggs, you will notice that they take more baths than usual. This is nature's way of keeping the eggs moist as the parents sit on the clutch.

If you hear the chick "chirping" inside the egg, you can expect it to hatch within twenty-four hours.

The egg will rock back and forth, and soon you will see a pinhole about a quarter of the way down from the wider end of the egg. The chick is using an egg tooth (located on the upper mandible) to peck its way out into the world. It will usually only have to peck about half way around the egg as the rest of the egg will break away due to all of the movement inside. This process could take just a few minutes or could take hours to complete.

When the chicks hatch, leave them in the incubator for at least eight hours; they are wet and must have time to dry. You will know when it is safe to remove them as their down will fluff out.

There is a "viewing" window on the top of the incubator, allowing you to witness the hatching and to keep an eye on the chicks until they are dry enough to go into a brooder

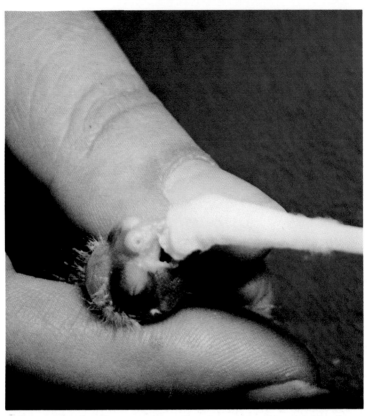

After each feeding session, gently wash the chick's face, especially in and around the mouth, with a cotton swab moistened with warm water. Remnants of food left inside the beak can cause irritation and thus prevent the chick from getting proper nourishment.

36

box. Do not open the incubator to remove the shells unless you see a chick in trouble.

I leave the chick in the incubator for at least eight hours and open the incubator only if the chick stumbles back into its shell where it could suffocate. The chick will stumble around and will fall on its back, not staying in the same spot for any length of time. It is looking for its mother and will soon cuddle up to one of the other eggs for a rest, and then will start to roam again. If another chick has already hatched, the chick will seek it out, and they will huddle together.

If the egg has not completely opened several hours after the time a hole was first formed in the shell, you should open the egg yourself, as the chick could suffocate. The newly hatched chick is fragile and has very thin skin. Needless to say, caution must be used when opening the shell.

THE BROODER BOX

The newly hatched chicks will live in a brooder box from the time they leave the incubator until they are feathered out at about four to five weeks old. Once they have their feathers, they can live in a cage quite comfortably. The feathers serve as a protective covering, preventing the bird from losing its body heat.

We built our brooder box with plywood and pegboard; however, you can use a shoe box if you have only one or two chicks to raise. If you are going to use a shoe box, be sure to punch "breathing" holes through the sides and top. Place the box on a heating pad and put a 40-watt light bulb over the box. The temperature should be maintained at between 80 and 90 F., being regulated with the controls of the heating pad. Put a folded hand towel on the bottom of the box and cover it with paper towels.

Making a wooden brooder box is a fairly simple task. To construct our box we bought a two-foot long heating element. The element didn't have a thermostat to regulate the heat, so my husband, Peter, connected a regular electrical dimmer switch to the wiring. He built a box of quarter-inch plywood, 2 ft. square by 1 ft. high. He attached the heating element just below the top edge, about 4 in. from the back of the box. An eighth-inch piece of peg board made a good sliding top. Using the peg board, it was not necessary to drill ventilation holes into the rest of the box.

Now that the box has been built, it's time to set up housekeeping. A regular bath towel folded in half is a good padding for the bottom. Cover the towel with paper towels for easy cleaning. A rolled-up hand towel on each end of the box gives the chicks something to snuggle up to. In the nest box, the chicks snuggle up to the parents, and the towels in the brooder box provide a good substitute. Hang a thermometer on the middle of one of the inside walls of the box. If the thermometer is left on the floor, the chicks are sure to soil it, and, worst of all, they could injure themselves while they are exploring their new home. If you keep the temperature in the middle of the brooder box at 85 F., the area under the heating element will be a few degrees warmer and the temperature at the other end of the box will be a few degrees cooler.

When the chicks first enter the box, they will seek out the warmest end of it. As the chicks become older and begin to feather out, you will see them wander towards the cooler end. You will always be able to tell where they have been because their droppings are sure to be left behind. Now you know why we use paper towels to cover the bath towels.

HAND-REARING

This is the hardest but most rewarding part of your new adventure. These little chicks are completely dependent on you for their survival. Those ugly, naked little cockatiel chicks are going to become gorgeous little birds right before your eyes. You will be amazed at how fast they grow in size and you literally will be able to watch the feathers grow.

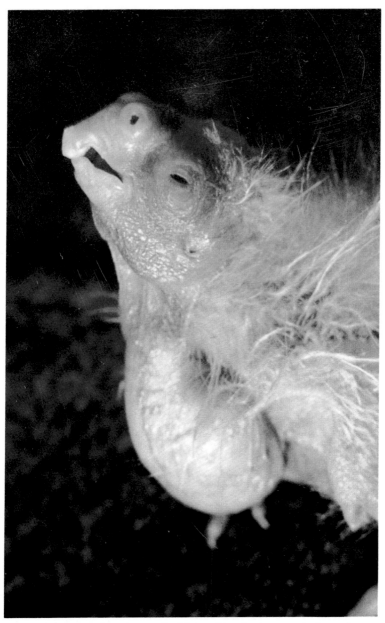

While feeding a hand-reared chick, offer just enough formula so that the crop appears full (above). Using the syringe method of feeding, several portions of formula can be kept warm by placing the syringes in a cup of hot water (opposite).

Place the newly hatched chicks together in the warmest end of the box. They will cuddle up to each other while snuggling up to the rolled-up hand towel. The chicks will chirp (actually more of a hissing sound) and stretch out their little necks to encourage you to feed them. Their hissing sound will become louder and sound more like a chirp as they get older; usually by the time they're five to six weeks old, their chirp will be loud and clear.

Don't worry about feeding the newborn chicks for the first few hours, as the parents don't feed them for about twelve hours. After twelve hours, the chicks will very quickly become dehydrated and will die. I give them their first feeding at about nine hours.

For the first four days, I use the following formula with excellent results:

½ cup high-protein baby cereal
½ cup wheat germ
½ cup bread crumbs
¼ pint plain yogurt
2 drops vitamins
1 hard-boiled egg
1 cup water

Puree the ingredients in an electric blender until it is a thick liquid. The yogurt is a good source of bacteria. Bacteria is needed in the digestive tract to aid in breaking down the food and making it available to the bird for absorption. The chick normally receives bacteria from the parent bird in the food that is regurgitated and then fed to it.

Do not store the formula for more than three days in the refrigerator. After the third day, if you have any formula left, discard it and whip up a new batch.

FEEDING TECHNIQUES

Prepare your feeding area as close to the brooder box as possible. Keeping the chicks away from the warmth of the box for any extra length of time could be dangerous. Cover your work area with a thick layer of toweling to prevent injuries to the chick if a fall should occur. Never let the young chick stand on a slippery surface as it will not be able to control its legs. The legs will slide out from under it. Its little feet are not strong enough yet to keep it from sliding. Once again, be sure that the chick is always on a soft surface.

You will need a bowl of hot water (by the time you use it, it will be warm), a box of cotton swabs, a clean, soft wash cloth, and a box of facial tissues. Fill a hypodermic syringe (without the needle) with the formula and place the syringe in a glass of hot water. By the time the water in the glass cools to warm, the formula will be ready for the chick. Test the formula on your wrist as you would for a baby. Never try to give the chick cold formula. First of all, it won't eat it, and, second and most important, the cold formula may sour its crop and cause many problems, usually ending up in death if not treated immediately.

There are different techniques for feeding the baby chicks. One way is to put a small amount of formula in an egg poacher and use an eye dropper for feeding. Another way is to use bowls in a double-boiler manner and use the eye dropper. I find the syringe to be best as the formula doesn't cool off as fast, and if there is more than one baby to feed, you can have another syringe keeping warm in the glass of water while you are feeding the other chick. There is less of a mess to clean up when using syringes because there isn't any formula exposed to the air to harden. If your chicks are of different ages and need separate formulas, you can heat the formulas all together if you take a permanent felt-tip marker to mark each of the syringes.

To save time when I have a lot of chicks to feed, I clean and refill the syringes after each feeding, store them in the refrigerator and have them ready to pop into hot water at the next feeding. Another advantage to doing it this way is always knowing ahead of time when you need to make more

Two four-day-old chicks alongside a newborn (above), and here the same chicks at seven and three days old. The eyes of the older birds have opened (below).

Before each feeding session, assemble all of the necessary equipment: a towel, a formula-filled syringe, a bowl of warm water, cotton swabs, a warm wash cloth, and facial tissues (above). There may be different feeding schedules and different formulas for each of the youngsters (below).

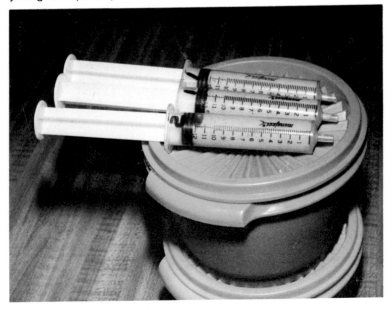

formula. The baby chicks are not about to wait happily for you to mix up a new batch of food when it's their feeding time.

Cockatiels do not open their mouths wide to be fed as do other birds. Put the tip of the syringe into the beak and gently feed the chick slowly while you hold its head between your thumb and index finger. The chick normally bobs its head up and down when being fed by the parents, and it's going to bob its head while you're feeding it, so hold it firmly and, of course, gently.

Within just a day or two, whenever you open the brooder box, the chicks will hiss at you to inform you that they are hungry and expect to be fed. If it is not feeding time, they will quiet down as soon as you close the box; however, if it is feeding time, they will all want to be fed first. I usually feed the youngest first, as it is the most impatient.

Try not to open the brooder box for the first few days (except, of course, for feeding) to show off the chicks. Your friends and neighbors will understand if you tell them how harmful a constant gush of cool air is to the babies. Your friends are only going to think that the chicks are ugly little things, but you and I know what beautiful creatures we can expect to have.

The chick will chirp while it is feeding, and seems to swallow more air than food. You will be able to see the air bubble forming in the crop as the skin is almost transparent. With your thumb and index finger, work the air up the neck. You will hear the chick burp; then continue feeding until the crop looks full. Do not over-feed. The crop should be full but not ready to burst. You may have to burp the chick more than once during feeding. If you are finished feeding the chick and can't get all of the air out of its crop, don't keep it out of the brooder box too long trying to burp it. A little air will not hurt it.

With a cotton swab and warm water (from the bowl of water you put near your work area) wash the chick's face and anywhere else that may have gotten soiled. Be sure to look inside its beak. Any food left to dry in the mouth can cause sore spots and other problems, including upset stomach, and sometimes the sore spots can prevent the chick from feeding at all.

After you have dried the chick with the soft wash cloth, put it back into the brooder box and take out the next one. You will be able to tell which chick has or has not been fed by the size of its crop. Never take more than one chick out of the box at a time for feeding, as they are easily chilled.

Now that all of the chicks have been fed, change the paper towels in the brooder box. The chicks' droppings are very soft; if left for them to walk through, this will make cleaning the chicks at mealtime more difficult. As the chicks get older and the feedings are at longer intervals, change the towels more often; don't wait for feeding time to change the paper towels.

For the first few days, you will be feeding the chicks every two to three hours. There is no need to feed them during the night. I start the first feeding of the day at 6 AM and give the last feeding at 11 PM. The chicks will naturally sleep during the night, and their crops will not be totally empty by morning, but during the day they exercise and will digest the food rapidly. Never let the crop get completely empty. When there is a small amount of formula in the crop, feed the chick immediately. By the time the chick is a week old, you will notice that the formula lasts longer, and you will be able to increase the hours between feedings to between four and six hours. Each bird is an individual and has its own needs. If one chick has a little food left in the crop, and another's is half full, feed them both.

There is no need to have different feeding schedules for the chicks. If you have a group of chicks with a large difference in ages, just skip the oldest ones a few of the feeding times, but feed them with the other, younger chicks during one of their normal mealtimes. This is where marking the

This eight-day-old chick is starting to lose the sheaths from its wing feathers (above). The same bird at nine days (below).

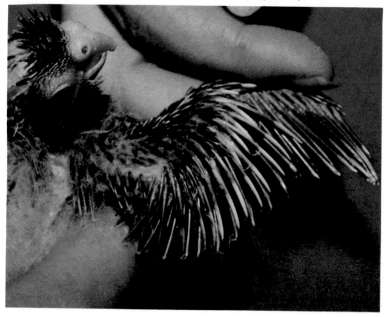

At eleven days, the wings of the chick are starting to take shape and to feather out (above). The wings are entirely feathered at fifteen days (below).

syringes comes in handy, as the older chicks will be on a different formula.

When the chicks are four days old, add to the original formula:

> ½ teaspoon brewer's yeast
> ½ teaspoon wheat germ oil

When a week old, add:

> ½ jar carrots (strained baby food)
> 1 tablespoon honey
> 2 tablespoons peanut butter (smooth)

After the second week, you can experiment by adding other vegetables, and even the strained meats. My cockatiel chicks thought that turkey was just great.

When the chicks are three weeks old, grind up ½ cup of budgerigar seed-mix and add it to your formula. This will give the chick the "taste" for seed. Take your feeding syringe and with a razor blade make a diagonal cut at the tip to widen the hole. The formula is thicker now, and the larger hole allows the mixture to flow easily. There is nothing worse, when feeding the chick, than having a seed stuck in the hole of the syringe and giving it a big squeeze to release the blockage. Now the poor hungry chick has not only a mouth full of formula, but it is dripping down its chest and onto its feet. The bird will now know what a complete bath is, as it is definitely going to need one.

WEANING THE CHICKS

Between the age of four to five weeks, the chicks are feathered out and are ready to face the world in their own cage. You have the chore of weaning them. It is hard to say no to that cute little chick that looks at its "mommy" and demands to be fed. If you are a pushover, that bird will have you hand-feed it until it's two years old. If you're stern, it will learn to eat on its own easily.

To get the chick interested in eating seeds, crack ¼ cup of budgerigar mix with a rolling pin. Do not crush the seeds. You will hear the seeds cracking under the rolling pin, but you will probably not be able to see the cracks in the hulls. Sprinkle these seeds and a little bit of grit on the bottom of the cage. Cracking the seeds makes it easier for the chick to learn how get to the kernel of the seed.

Mix up a batch of formula, grinding only the budgerigar mix. Do not puree the mixture in the blender any more. You are now making a mash and will not be using the syringes. Mix all of the ingredients by hand.

I find that if you take a plastic quarter-teaspoon and warm it over an open flame, you can take a pair of pliers and squeeze the tip of the spoon into a "V" shape. The new shape of the spoon is readily accepted by the chick as it is as close to the shape of the mother's beak as we can get. Once again you will have to hold the chick's head during feeding, for it will still bob it up and down, causing the food to go everywhere except in its mouth.

Always warm the mash before feeding the chicks. Put more than what you will need for the feeding into a small bowl that is not easily tipped over. Feed the chick with the spoon and put the bowl with the remaining mash into the cage. Be sure to change the mash at least twice a day. If the food is allowed to turn rancid, it will surely kill the chicks. Freshness of the mash is most important. The mash in the cage will teach the chicks how to feed from a dish.

Hanging millet spray on the side of the cage so that the end of it just touches the bottom of the cage will entice the chick to peck at it. If the millet spray is set on the bottom of the cage the chick will cuddle up to it and only sleep on it, not knowing that it is food. A rolled up soft wash cloth makes a nice little pillow for the chick until it starts to stand

Even at five weeks, the chick will jerk its head while being fed and cause the formula to go everywhere but in its mouth. The above chick can expect a face, neck, and chest bath to follow its recent meal.

Opposite:
Two methods of hand feeding formula: with the syringe (above) and with a plastic spoon that has been heated and shaped into a "V" (below).

on the perch. Once the chick learns to use the perch, it will lose all interest in the pillow.

With the chick being out in the open in its cage, it will keep its eye on you whenever possible. This is the time that it will learn how the world around it lives. While it was in the brooder box, it saw you only when you were either feeding it or changing the paper towels. Now it will learn that life is not just eating and sleeping.

Be sure to have the toys in the cage low enough for the chick to reach, remembering that it is on the floor and toys hung from the top of the cage will be 'way out of reach for it. At first it may be afraid of its new playthings, but after inspecting and tasting them, it will learn that its cage is a fun place for it to be. It may hiss when it first hears the sound of the toy bell, but soon you will see it playing with it and getting under it, pushing its head into it and using it as a hat.

Set up the baby cage as explained before. Sprinkle a few sunflower seeds on the bottom of the cage with the grit and the cracked budgie mix. The sunflower seeds make great new toys for the chick. It will pick them up and carry them around in its mouth, with its head held high. Soon it will learn to crack the shell and eat the kernel. Within a week or so it will be eating only its "adult" food. Your chick has been weaned.

You know that your chick is weaned, but the chick doesn't. It still thinks that you are only there to hand-feed it. If it cries for food whenever it sees you, try taking it out of the cage and away from its feeding area. Sit down with it and let it walk around and explore new areas. It will soon forget its appetite and enjoy its new experience as a bird, not a baby. After a few days, it will know that you are there for love and playing, as well as for keeping food and water in its cage.

FROM THE EGG
TO THE CAGE

This chapter is a day-to-day diary of one of the chicks that I hatched in an incubator. I am using this particular chick because he seemed to follow a normal growth pattern. Not all chicks grow at this pace; some are faster and some are slower. This will give you a general idea of what to expect as your chick grows.

DAY ONE: The chick is born. How ugly with his bulging eyes, bald head, chubby wet body, and stringy little legs! His chirp is more of a squeak than the sound of a bird. He eats well and doesn't mind having his little face washed and dried.

DAY TWO: Starting at 6 AM, the feedings are every two hours until midnight. After one of the feedings, it took so long to burp the chick I returned him to the brooder box with a little air left in his crop, figuring that it was better to let him have a little bubble in his crop than to let him catch cold being away from the box too long. At the next feeding I was able to remove all of the air.

DAY THREE: The chick is standing with better control of his legs; he's a good strong chick. He is eating well. While I was cleaning out the inside of his mouth, he discovered that the wet cotton swab wasn't food. Now he doesn't like to be washed and dried.

The eyelids are starting to form on this four-day-old nestling. In a few days, the eyes will completely open.

Opposite:
Feather development is underway for this eight-day-old chick. They eyes have opened and the legs are able to support the youngster for short intervals (above). The remarkable growth pattern is evident here with a five-week-old, two eight-day-old chicks, and a four-day-old (below).

DAY FOUR: The crop isn't getting empty as fast; put him on a three-hour feeding schedule. When the three hours are over, his crop isn't completely empty so I'll keep him on this schedule for a few days. His eyes are starting to open, as the eyelids develop.

DAYS FIVE and SIX: Quills on the wings are developing. He is more than twice the size he was at birth. His eyes are almost completely open.

DAY SEVEN: The pin feathers are developing on his neck, his back, and on his head. His face is getting a darker color around the eyes. The eyes are completely open, and now, when I open the box, he is hissing for food. He now knows me as "mommy," and "mommy" means food.

DAY EIGHT: All of the feathers are growing everywhere; even the tail is there. He has doubled in size again. I am able to put him on a five-hour feeding schedule, as he is taking in more food and it is lasting a bit longer.

DAYS NINE to ELEVEN: The sheaths are coming off the feathers. The more I touch him, the more sheaths are left on the towel. Now when I put him on the towel, he walks toward the syringe; he knows where his food is kept.

DAYS TWELVE to FOURTEEN: At two weeks old, this chick thinks he's a full-grown cockatiel, trying to flap his little wings. The feathers are getting longer and longer as each day passes. There is a flurry of feather sheaths all over the towels in the brooder box, as he is now wandering around exploring every inch of the box.

DAY FIFTEEN: A six-hour feeding schedule is called for, as his crop is still far from empty. The crop has started to shrink as the feathers grow in to cover it. He still gulps down his food and hates to have his face washed and dried.

DAYS SIXTEEN to EIGHTEEN: Now when I open the brooder box, the chick tries to jump out. He must be tired of living in the dark and is beginning to look forward to his time out in the cooler air. I dropped the temperature in the box to 75 F., as he spends most of his time at the cooler end of the box. His droppings are a dead giveaway as to where he's been.

DAYS NINETEEN to TWENTY-ONE: Feathers have grown, most of the sheaths are off, and his feeding time has increased to eight hours. It is time for him to leave the box and have his very own cage. The perch is close to the floor so that when he falls from it he won't hurt himself. The first few times I put him on the perch, he immediately fell. By the end of the day he was standing on the perch for twenty minutes at a time.

DAYS TWENTY-TWO to TWENTY-FOUR: He is becoming interested in the cracked seeds on the bottom of the cage. I am now feeding him only twice a day, at 7 AM and at 7 PM. He is standing on the perch for longer periods of time without falling off, and he steps on and off it by himself. Stretching and flapping his wings seems to be great fun.

DAYS TWENTY-FIVE to TWENTY-SEVEN: He now cries whenever I feed the younger chicks, hoping that maybe this is his time to eat. As soon as I finish feeding the chicks and walk away, he stops his crying and waits for the next time.

DAYS TWENTY-EIGHT to THIRTY: He's eating his cracked seeds often, but when I walk up to the cage, he drops the seed and cries for me to get the syringe. I talk to

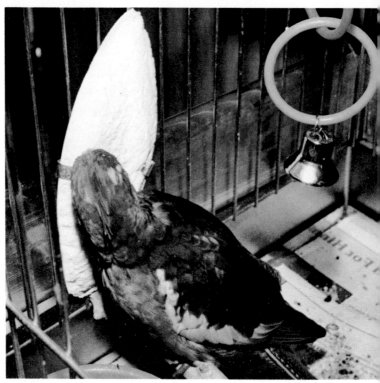

Perches should be placed near the bottom of the cage for a newly weaned chick so that it can learn to balance itself while feeding and nibbling on cuttlebone.

Opposite:
It is time for this six-week-old cockatiel to change over to a primarily all-seed diet. This is its last syringe feeding (above). Color markings, the well-developed upper and lower mandible, and even eyelashes are apparent on this healthy six-week-old specimen (below).

him for a few minutes, then take him out of the cage and play for a while. When he is returned, he forgets about the syringe and continues to eat seeds.

DAYS THIRTY-ONE to THIRTY-THREE: His hand-feeding is now down to once a day at 3 PM. I still haven't seen him drink water, but it is disappearing faster than it could evaporate, and I know that he's not spilling it.

DAYS THIRTY-FOUR to THIRTY-SIX: He climbs up that ladder like an old pro. I watched him fall off the high perch and run back up the ladder to continue playing with his toys. He still doesn't want me to catch him eating seeds, so he drops them when he sees me.

DAYS THIRTY-SEVEN to THIRTY-NINE: He took his first flight around the living room, and now I can clip his wing feathers. His first flight after having his wings clipped was from the coffee table to the floor. He was very happy with his short flight, and enjoyed the freedom of the room.

I finally caught him eating the seeds from his dish (these seeds aren't cracked for him) and drinking water. This chick is weaned; no more syringe. Now he doesn't stop eating when I walk up to the cage, and there is no more crying; he has learned to chirp instead. This little chick is now a full-fledged, happy little bird.

As I said in the beginning, not all chicks will grow at this pace. Some will be faster and some will be slower. It is a great feeling when you know that with your help this little creature survived the most critical time of his life.

HAND-TAMING
AND TALKING

HAND-TAMING

The chick you just weaned doesn't need hand-taming as it considers you to be its mother and is not frightened by the human hand. This section applies to the newly purchased cockatiel.

The younger the cockatiel is, the easier it will be to hand tame it, but no matter how old a bird is, it can be hand tamed. Naturally an older bird will take longer to tame than a younger one, but with proper handling, both will become loving, adorable pets that you will be proud to have in your home.

When you first bring home your cockatiel, put its cage in the busiest room of the house, except for the kitchen. The temperature in a kitchen will vary too much because of cooking and the use of the back door. For the first day, don't go near the cage. The cockatiel knows that it is in a strange place and is quite aware of anyone being near its area. It will be afraid of all of the strange noises around, but soon will realize that the commotion is not harmful. You will know that it feels safe and secure when you can walk into the room while it is eating and it ignores you.

During the second day, walk up to the cage and talk softly to the bird while you're changing its food and water. Continue talking as you clean the bottom of the cage and the perches. Leave the cage for just a few minutes; then

The taming and training of your cockatiel must be built on a mutual trust between bird and keeper. Always approach your pet slowly and speak to it in a quiet, soothing tone of voice.

Opposite:
In just a few days, with patience, you can train your pet cockatiel to step onto your finger (above), and onto a perch (below).

return and slowly—while still talking in a soothing tone of voice—open the cage door and slip in a millet spray. Leave your hand in the cage for a few minutes without trying to touch the bird. It will flutter around to let you know that it doesn't like the intruding hand. Remove your hand while still talking to it. Walk away from the cage, but stay near enough for the bird to keep an eye on you. Be sure to continue talking to it.

Go back in a few minutes and place your hand into the cage. If the bird is still nervous, carefully cup your hand around its back and put your other hand under it. Take it out of the cage while calming it with your voice and bring it to a quiet room. We use our bedroom, where we place a towel on the bed. Be sure that all of the windows are closed. By kneeling next to the bed you can make a circle around the bird with your arms. Each time the cockatiel tries to leave the "corral," slip your hand under it and return it to the center. Soon, when you go to return it, it will stand on your finger. Within a half hour or so it should be calming down and will stay on your finger.

Now that the bird is comfortable on your finger, put the index finger of your other hand in front of it. If it doesn't readily step onto your other finger, give it a little nudge under the chest to get it moving. Continue this for a few minutes until it is comfortable walking your finger "ladder."

Do not forget to continually talk to it with a soothing voice. Never yell at it to scold it during training. Your attitude is very important to successfully train your bird. If you don't train the bird with ease and confidence, it will be aware of it and will become nervous. If both you and the bird are nervous, don't expect an easy training lesson. It must be able to feel that it can thoroughly trust you; after all, look how much bigger you are compared to it! Believe me, it's more frightened of you than you ever could be of it. This poor little creature was literally stolen from its parents and locked up in a cage. All it wants from you is a lot of love and affection, and, of course, food, water, and a clean cage.

Always reward its progress with a special treat. Be sure to have treats on hand, particularly during the training period.

At your next training session, take the bird out of the cage on your finger and walk around the room while talking to it. Your soft, soothing voice will reassure it that there isn't any danger. With your free hand, try stroking the top of its head. If it resists your hand, take it to a mirror; it will see the other bird having its head stroked and will tolerate it better. Of course all of its attention will not be on itself, as it will be aware of the reflection in the mirror. Soon you will be able to pat its head, neck, and back.

If the cockatiel should become startled while out of its cage, it will take flight. Never try to catch it while it is flying as you can do quite a bit of damage, including breaking its wings. Let it land and then, while talking to it calmly, go to it and let it step up onto your finger. While taking it back to the cage, talk softly to let it know that everything is all right.

After a few training periods, instead of putting it inside the cage, let the bird get on top of it. This lets it know that it is as safe outside its cage as it is inside. So far, the only time it has been away from its cage it has been with you, and you have been its protection. Soon it will learn that your house is as safe as its home.

Your cockatiel will look forward to having you come to the cage, as this means more freedom. If you plan to leave it out of the cage all day, make sure that there is food and water on the playground. Always be sure that it is put back into its cage whenever you leave the house and at night. The cage is its security, and any strange noise will trigger it into flight if it is out of its cage. Flying like this could send

A pet cockatiel must be tamed before it can be expected to mimic words and sounds or to learn tricks.

Opposite:
Like Ann Bulger, other children can learn to tame their pet birds. The extended index finger becomes a place for the bird to perch (above), and by placing one index finger in front of the other, the bird will learn to "step up the ladder" (below).

69

it into walls or windows, knocking it unconscious or even killing it.

If at any time during training it really tries to bite you, try blowing on its face and tell it, "No." It will quickly stop this biting practice. Your tone of voice will let it know that it is doing something wrong, and that you don't like it. There is no reason to yell or raise your voice.

After every training lesson, it is best to offer the bird a treat of apple, carrot, or any other special food it likes. This lets it know that it did well, and it will look forward to each training session.

No matter how well-trained your bird is, never take it outdoors unless the wing feathers are clipped, or it is in a cage. If you do take your cockatiel outside, do not put it in direct sunlight. Always let it have plenty of shade. Too much sun will dehydrate it quickly. Make sure that there is drinking water available. If it isn't going to be outdoors all day, it can wait until it returns indoors for its food.

THE TALKING COCKATIEL

Both male and female cockatiels are good talkers, but the male seems to be able to whistle a longer tune than the female. Teaching more than one cockatiel to talk is almost impossible, as they will be more interested in each other than in learning. Be sure to remove all mirrors from the cage. If you don't, the bird will be too busy admiring itself to pay attention to you.

Birds do not understand the words; they listen to the vibrations. The higher the vibration, the quicker the cockatiel will learn. It is best to have a woman or a child teach the bird, as their voices are usually pitched higher than a man's. If you listen to any of the pet-training recordings, you will find that they have been done by women.

Cockatiel training records and tapes are found in the pet shops. These recordings are made to aid you in training the bird to talk. Do not use the recordings exclusively. Many people have found that if the training is entirely left to the recordings, the cockatiel will talk only when it is alone because it was the only one in the room while it was learning. If you want to use the recordings as an aid, you should not use them more often than every other training time. Be sure that you use the exact words that are on the records or tapes. Whenever you go near the cage, talk to the cockatiel, using the lesson words for the day.

Repetition is the key for any training. Each day inform the members of your family which words to speak to the bird, as the more it hears each word, the quicker it will learn it. There is no set time for when the bird will learn its first word, as each bird has its own learning ability. You will find that after it masters the first word, other words will be learned in shorter periods of time.

Sometimes your friends can be helpful with the training, but you may run into someone who wants to teach your pet special words. I once had a friend who thought it would be "cute" to teach my cockatiel a few dirty words. Be careful, as the birds seem to pick up these words very quickly. Needless to say, if you have friends with that type of humor, let them know what kind of words you want your bird to learn.

Vitamins can be added to the cockatiel's drinking water; however, one should administer vitamins by hand to a sick bird.

GROOMING AND
HEALTH PROBLEMS

WING CLIPPING

Clipping the wing feathers of your cockatiel is not cruel, nor does it hurt. Having feathers clipped is like humans having their hair cut. Clipping prevents it from flying into things and becoming injured.

Some people clip just one wing. Clipping the one wing will prevent the bird from flying in the direction it aims for, as one full wing will set its flight in a curve. When the bird realizes that it can't fly to its chosen destination, it will soon stop trying.

Others will clip both wings to allow the bird to have a more balanced appearance. Then when the bird tries to fly, it will fly down to the floor, but in a straight line.

Leaving the first two primary flight feathers and clipping the rest is the most widely used method. These feathers act as a support for the new feathers to grow against. Without any support, the new feathers may grow in weak or break at the quill. The first two primary feathers also protect the new feathers from being picked at. As the new feathers grow in, the bird will have a tendency to chew on them. If the outside feathers are there it is difficult for the bird to get at the new ones, and it will soon forget them and will peck at its toys instead.

Never clip the primary flight feathers closer to the wing than the ends of the primary coverts. The primary coverts are the row of shorter feathers along the wing that overlap the flight feathers. If the primary flight feathers are cut below the coverts and if one of the quills should split, an ingrown feather may result. The extra room allowed by the coverts is usually enough to prevent these ingrown feathers.

When you purchase your cockatiel, have the seller clip the wings while you watch. By having him do it, you will have your first lesson in handling the bird. Be sure to pay attention because new feathers will grow in, and they will have to be clipped again in a few months.

CLIPPING CLAWS

Clipping the cockatiel's claws is essential to its health. If the claws are left to grow too long, the bird will not be able to stand on its perch properly and may come to have foot problems.

By clipping just the tip of each claw about once a month with a pair of regular toenail clippers, you should not have any problems. If you wait until the claw gets too long, you will run the risk of clipping the blood vessel that runs through the claw. The longer the claw is allowed to grow, the longer the vein will grow.

If you should clip the claw too short and it begins to bleed, apply Kwik-Stop to the end of the claw. The bleeding should stop immediately; if it does not, apply the Kwik-Stop again. When the bleeding stops, place the bird on its perch in the cage and every few minutes check to make sure that the bleeding has not recurred. If the bird is very active, it could scrape the end of the claw and start the bleeding again.

You can try using emery boards on the claws; just a few strokes on each will do the job. The bird may not like having his claws filed, and the clippers are much quicker to use. However, if you spend a lot of time holding and playing with your cockatiel, it may let you file a claw or two in one sitting. This is time-consuming and will work well if you can do at least one foot each time. You don't want to be continually working on your bird's feet; if you do, the bird will associate you with just having its feet worked on. Any time you have to work on any part of the cockatiel's body, try to do your job as quickly as possible.

Reward the bird with its favorite treat any time you have to clip its claws or work on it in any way. You want it to remember the treat, not the work that was done.

TRIMMING THE BEAK

An overgrown beak is a common disorder among caged birds. In the wild, the beak is kept under control as the bird chews at the bark on trees. In the cage, the constant scraping on the cuttlebone helps keep the beak from growing out of control.

Occasionally you may have to trim the beak because the bird does not use it as much in the cage as it would in the wild. It doesn't have to scrape around looking for food or grit; it is all there in its cage. Trimming the beak is done as easily as clipping the claws. Use your toenail clippers and just trim the point of the beak. There is a blood supply to the beak as to the claws. After trimming the beak, use an emery board to smooth any rough spots.

Beak trimming could be a traumatic experience for the bird. When you have finished working on it, place it in the cage so it can rest.

POSSIBLE PROBLEMS

Your cockatiel could live a long and healthy life without ever becoming ill. If it has the proper diet, vitamins, a clean cage, proper care, and a lot of loving attention, it will reward you with all its love and devotion.

If it should have a problem, your pet dealer may be able to help you by recommending which treatment to use and how to use it. Your veterinarian is your bird's family doc-

A cockatiel that is to be let out of its cage should have one of its wings clipped. One person should hold the extended wing (above), while the other person clips some of the primary flight feathers (below).

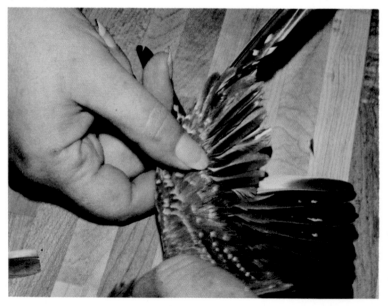

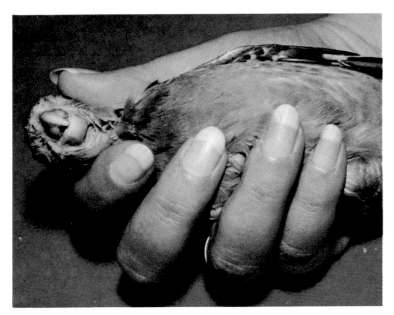

By holding the cockatiel in this manner, one can inspect the bird's general health (above). In this same position, using a regular toenail clipper, the bird's claws can be clipped. Snip only the tip off each claw (below).

tor, so don't be afraid to call him. A health problem which looks hopeless to you may very well be successfully treated by the veterinarian.

If the bird is bleeding and you can't staunch the flow, don't waste time; just get the bird to the veterinarian. Your bird is small, and a few drops of its blood is equivalent to a pint of ours.

COLDS: Colds in birds are caused by a virus just as they are in humans; however, a human cannot catch a cold from a bird. Some of the cold symptoms are the same as in humans: stuffy or runny nostrils, sneezing, lack of appetite, difficulty in breathing, and feeling just plain miserable. The bird will be listless, often have watery eyes, and will ruffle up its feathers. If you don't notice the cold in its early stages, the bird will quickly develop other problems, especially pneumonia.

Place the bird in a hospital cage with the temperature at 80 to 85 F. If its nostrils are caked with mucus, use a wet, warm cotton ball to soften and clear it. You can use an "over-the-counter" inhalant to keep its nasal passages clear. Following the package directions, put a respiratory medication (found in your pet shop) in its water. If its appetite worsens or it doesn't seem to be improving within a couple of days, do not hesitate; call your veterinarian.

BLEEDING: If the cockatiel has had the misfortune to cut itself, do not despair. Apply a styptic pencil or Kwik-Stop to the wound. Within a matter of seconds the bleeding should stop; if not, repeat the procedure.

Your bird may from time to time break one of its primary feathers by flying into the side of its cage, falling off the perch, or just getting into things around the house. If it has broken the feather so that it bleeds, pull the broken quill from the wing. It is very rare for blood to leak from the skin where the quill was. A new feather will grow in its place.

A little common sense is needed when it comes to "doctoring" your pet bird. Never apply any medication to or near the eye without specific instruction from your veterinarian. If the bird has quite a gash and is bleeding profusely, don't waste any time trying to fix it yourself; get the bird to your veterinarian. This section is meant to be followed only for minor bleeding problems.

UNCONSCIOUSNESS: If your bird should fly into a wall or window, knocking itself unconscious, wrap it in a dry, soft wash cloth and keep it warm. When it is feeling better, return it to the cage for the rest of the day. As soon as possible, clip its wings to prevent another flying accident.

If you leave your bird out of its cage when you are out of the house, or at night when everyone is in bed asleep, you are just looking for trouble. Remember, even if the cocktiel's wings are clipped, it will still try to fly away if it hears a strange noise, as, for example, the sudden screeching of a car's brakes. This is a sudden noise breaking up the silence of the home. Even with its wings clipped, the bird can get itself into trouble flying down onto furniture.

SHOCK: Whenever you suspect that the bird has gone into shock, the best thing you can do is to put it into the hospital cage and keep it warm.

Shock can be caused by a number of things, anything from a change in temperature to the bird surviving an accident. This is why, when showing signs of shock, the first forty-eight hours are so critical; if the bird becomes further stressed, it could die.

Each bird has its own emotional level. A bird that is "high-strung" may over-react to something that another bird may take for granted as normal. Stress is an environmental factor that has an adverse effect on the adrenal glands.

When the bird is in shock, it will stand almost lifeless either on its perch or on the bottom of the cage. It will lose

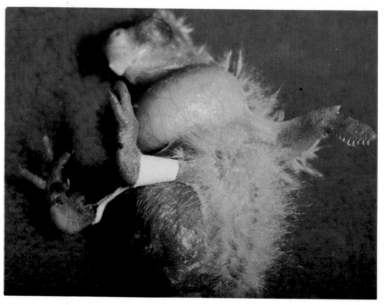

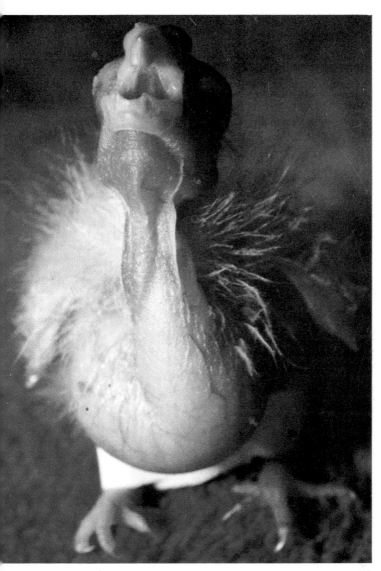

A condition known as "spraddle legs" affects some chicks, whereby the legs spread out to the sides (opposite, above). If caught early enough, this problem can be corrected by simply taping the chick's legs together (opposite, below) so that they remain straight, in a standing position (above). The tape should be kept in place for a few days and removed only once daily for about an hour.

all interest in food and water, and ignore its cuttlebone and toys. Do not hesitate; put it in the hospital cage and set the temperature at 85 to 90 F. Heat is the best treatment for shock. If you don't notice an improvement in a day, call your veterinarian.

LICE AND MITES: Lice and mites will attack cage birds if they get a chance. Any cage you bring into your home should be thoroughly washed and dried before coming in contact with any bird. A brand-new cage could become infested while on the shelf in the store.

Red mites are the most common mites that attack cage birds. You will probably never see them in the daytime as they are gray in color (until they ingest blood) and hide in the cracks of wood, under the cage paper, in the corners of the cage, and other such places. The little pests will attack your bird only when the lights are turned off. If you suspect that your bird is infested with mites, cover its cage with a light-colored cloth and turn off the lights. After a couple of hours, quickly turn on the lights and remove the cloth. If there are mites, you will see little specks of gray or reddish color on the underside of the cloth.

Remember that the mites hide all over the cage during the day, so in all probability the mites will not be on the bird. Remove the bird from the cage. Soak the cage in the bathtub in hot water and a good disinfectant. After soaking it, scrub it down thoroughly, rinse it, and set it out in the sun to dry. Be sure to scrub everything that was in the cage, including the perches, food dishes, and toys. After the cage dries, use a mite spray (available in the pet shop) on the cage and the perches. When the cage is dry again, replace the perches, toys, and food dishes. Spray the bird and return it to the cage. Treat the bird's play areas in the same manner. Even though you know that you did a great job getting rid of the mites, once a week for a month use the mite spray on the cage and perches.

Feather lice are small, but you will be able to see them, as they eat the feather and lay their eggs along the shaft of the feather. Use the same treatment as for mites, but remember that the eggs will hatch and you will have to continue the treatment until all of the lice are gone.

DIRTY FEET: In the beginning, I told you that cleanliness is one of the most important ways to ensure your pet's good health. By being sure that you clean the bottom of the cage daily and the perches weekly, you will prevent the most frequent causes of dirty feet. The cockatiel likes to peck at the bottom of the cage, and it cannot do it unless it walks around on the paper. If the bird is constantly stepping in its droppings, its feet will become crusty and will develop sores. The bird literally lives standing on its feet twenty-four hours a day, and if there are sores on those little feet, its life will be miserable—not to mention the medical problems that will arise.

If its feet are soiled, offer it a bath first. If it refuses to bathe, you will have to take over. With warm water and a soft cloth try gently cleaning its feet. If the feet are really crusty, soak them for a few minutes, and then try again until they come clean.

SPRADDLE LEGS: If caught early enough (when the chick is just a few days old) spraddle legs can sometimes be corrected, although there is no guarantee that the treatment will work for all birds.

Two possible causes for spraddle legs are: First—after hatching the eggs the parents might sit on the chick too hard, causing its legs to spread out to the sides. Second—if the chick is allowed to remain on a slippery surface, the weight of its body will cause the feet to slide out from under it. The possibilty of spraddle legs being hereditary has been neither proven nor disproven.

This formerly spraddle-legged chick (above) had its legs taped for four days. Now it is able to stand normally with the legs close to the body. The same chick (opposite) at three weeks. One would never guess that this healthy, active cockatiel had spraddle legs.

Do not just place a piece of tape around the chick's legs; you must remember how thin-skinned and fragile they are. Taking a piece of cotton and wrapping each leg before taping will prevent the tape from sticking to or cutting the legs. Tape the legs together just above the ankle so that the legs are in a straight, standing position. If the tape is touching the stomach, very carefully cut the tape in a "U" shape to clear that area. Don't try to protect the stomach with cotton as this will only slip off, and even if it stayed secure, within minutes it would become soiled from the chick's droppings.

Each day remove the tape and let the chick exercise its legs for an hour or so. Replace the tape until the legs are straightened. You should see an improvement within three to four days. When you feel that it is safe to remove the tape, continue to check the untaped legs for a week to make sure that the condition has not returned. Above all, make sure that the chick is not allowed to stand on a slippery surface until he is weaned.

SOUR CROP: Sour crop is caused by undigested food in the crop. When food is left in a dark, damp, and warm environment, fungus will grow, which is a source of infection. Sour crop is very noticeable as the crop will be bulging with food, and an unusual odor will quickly be detected. The crop must be emptied.

To empty the crop, hold the bird upside down and work the food up the neck as if you were burping it. If the bird is not held upside down, the food will get into its lungs and surely will kill it. Keep working on the bird until all of the food is expelled from the crop. The bird may go into such shock that it will kill it, but if the food isn't removed, it is sure to die.

Flush out the crop with a solution of a teaspoon of bicarbonate of soda to ¼ cup of warm water, using a syringe with a narrow tube inserted down into the crop. Remove the water in the same way you removed the food. Three flushings should thoroughly clean the crop. Call your vet for antibiotics and further treatments.

THE HOSPITAL CAGE

If you have a brooder box, you can easily turn it into a hospital cage by removing the wooden front and inserting a wire-mesh front. The mesh will allow the bird to see outside. The brooder box is already equipped with a heater, so you won't have to use a heating pad on the bottom. After using it as a hospital cage, you can replace the wire with the original wooden front. Using the brooder box as a hospital cage eliminates having to have a spare cage handy.

If your bird should catch a cold or get sick, you will want to put it into a separate cage away from any other birds. The hospital cage can be any type of cage that is suitable for the cockatiel. To supply heat you can set a heating pad on the floor of the cage (covered to protect it from becoming soiled), or set the cage directly on the pad, which prevents the bird from coming in contact with the pad itself. Regulate the heat in the cage with the controls of the heating pad, and if more heat is needed, carefully hang a 25-watt light bulb at the top of the cage. Be sure that the wire is unreachable for the bird. Remove all of the perches and set the food, water, and grit dishes on the cage floor. Lower the cuttlebone and mineral block to a level the bird will be able to reach without having to stretch.

Cover three sides and the top of the cage with a light-colored cloth to hold in the heat. Leave the front of the cage uncovered so that the bird doesn't spend all day and night alone in the dark. Being able to look around the room and seeing you will give it a psychological lift.

If you have placed the bird in a hospital cage without first consulting your veterinarian and the ailing bird hasn't improved in a few days, seek professional help. You may be treating a symptom, and not the problem.

A plastic seed guard around the perimeter of the cage bottom helps to prevent seeds and their hulls from scattering all over the place.

HELPFUL HINTS

There are many things you can do to keep down the cost of having a happy bird in your home, and a few little tricks to make cleaning easier.

Cockatiels like to throw their seeds around. If I didn't know better I would think that they have their own little contest to see who can throw the seed the farthest. If you keep their cage in a carpeted room, try putting a sheet of plastic under and around the bottom of the cage. Those little seeds are a terror to get out of a carpet, and the plastic guard will catch most of them. Some cockatiel cages are equipped with three-inch pieces of plastic that slip onto the sides of the cage at the bottom. This helps a little, but the birds find a way to fling the seeds up and over the plastic shield.

You can purchase a playground for your bird in the pet shop, or you can save some money by building your own. If you build your own, use natural branches and your imagination. How about a nice, heavy formica base? We came across the perfect base in a lumber store. If the store makes custom counter tops, they have to cut out a good-sized section of the counter top to accommodate the sink. These cutouts are worthless to them, and you can get them for nothing, or next to nothing. You may have to ask the store manager for them, as sometimes they are just thrown away. If they are ordinarily tossed out, the manager will be happy to save one for you.

You can make your own custom playground with swings, ladders, hanging toys, and even a built-in bath tub. As I said, use your imagination, and by the time you're done, you will have a bird's paradise.

If you have extra food and water cups, you can save steps when cleaning the cage. By bringing fresh food and water to the cage, you can just exchange the cups and clean the cage in one trip.

Instead of cutting newspaper daily to fit the bottom of the cage, take a Sunday paper and cut all of the pages to size. You will be surprised at how long it will be before you have to cut more papers. I use a felt-tip marker and indicate on the bottom page of the stack of cut papers how much has to be cut off so I don't have to measure the cage each time I run out of papers.

Covering your cockatiel at night lets it know that it's bed-time. If it gets noisy during the day when you want it to be quiet, cover the cage. It will soon quiet down. Remove the cover, and if it continues to be noisy again, re-cover it. Soon it will learn that if it's quiet, it will be covered only at night.

When you go to bed at night, open the cover on the cage just a little bit. Even when the lights are turned off, a little natural light fills the room. If the bird has a little of this light in its cage and should it be frightened during the night, it will be able to see just enough so that it doesn't blindly bang around inside the cage.

Always give your pet its bath in the morning, and only if the sun is shining. This is more natural. If it is given a bath in the afternoon or at night, it will take longer to dry. A bird dries more slowly on cloudy days, and the quicker it dries, the less chance it has to get a chill.

Parsley is poison. This is one green that will quickly kill a bird. Humans use it mainly as a garnish in small amounts and would have to eat two pounds of parsley to be affected by the poison, but, once again, the bird is so small that just a little bit will do it in.

CONCLUSION

If you have learned just one thing that you previously didn't know about the cockatiel, I feel that I did a good job in writing this book.

Now that your bird loves and trusts you, you can expect to have a devoted companion for ten to fourteen years. It will be more than happy to sit on your shoulder while you are walking, standing, or sitting down relaxing.

It is said that birds do not have a memory, but they seem to remember anyone who has handled them roughly or mistreated them. Cockatiels are not born "mean"; they are born untamed. If someone tries to tell you that his bird is just plain mean, you can quess what kind of treatment the bird has received. If you acquire a mistreated bird, with a lot of loving care and your calm soothing tone of voice, it too will become a loving pet. It will take longer to train, but once it is trained, it will be devoted to you for life.

Once you have become a bird owner you may want to consider joining a bird club. Your pet store or veterinarian can tell you how to get in touch with one in your area. Basically, the bird club consists of people like yourself. A group of bird owners get together and share the experiences they have had with their birds, pet shops, veterinarians, and any new information on the care and raising of their pets. The club will have guest speakers from time to time. They will speak on different aspects of breeding and raising many types of birds. You will learn about new procedures for treating and caring your bird.

A pair of Cinnamon cockatiels. Fanciers who want to experiment with breeding the various color mutations, and who want successful results, must study the basic genetic principles, develop a plan of action, acquire good breeding stock, and record all pertinent data.

Opposite:
Another well-known mutation among
cockatiels is the Pearl. These birds are
characterized by whitish-yellow dappling
throughout their plumage.

Index

Age for breeding, 18
Antibiotics, 87
Appetite, lack of, 78, 82
Artificial incubation, 22, 34-8

Bacteria, 42
Bark, 14, 75
Bathing, 7, 19, 35, 83, 90
Beak trimming, 75
Behavior, 7, 54, 59, 63, 79, 91
  mating, 18-19
Bicarbonate of soda, 86
Biting, 18, 70
Bleeding, 74, 78-9
Branch, tree, 14, 89
Brooder box, 35-9, 46, 54, 87
Budgerigar seed mix, 50, 54

Cage cleaning, 11, 22, 82-3, 90
Cage placement, 11, 63
Candling, 22-3
Changing food and water, 11, 22,
  27, 63
Claw clipping, 74-5
Cleanliness, 7, 11, 15, 82-3
Clutch, 19, 31, 34-5
Cockatiel seed mix, 11
Colds, 11, 27, 78, 89
Color varieties, 15
Copulation, 18-19, 23
Courtship behavior, 18-19
Crop, 43, 46-7, 55, 58, 86-7
Cuttlebone, 11, 22, 75, 87

Dampness, 14
Death, causes of, 11, 14, 23, 26,
  35, 42-3, 51, 70, 79, 86
Dehydration, 26, 42, 70
Digestion, 42, 47
Dirty feet, 83
Drafts, 11, 14, 23, 31
Droppings, 10-11, 22, 39, 47, 59,
  83, 86

Egg laying, 10, 15, 19
Egg binding, 19
Eggs, turning the, 34-5
Egg tooth, 35
Exercise, 14, 47, 86
Eyes, puffy, 10

Feather development, 39, 58-9
Feather plucking, 34, 73
Feeding, 18, 26, 42-54
Feeding schedule, 34, 47, 55-9
Flight, 62, 67-70
Fostering, 31-4
Fruit, 11

Greenfood, 11, 91
Grit, 11, 26, 51, 54, 75
Grooming, 18
Growth, 39, 55-62

Handling, 63, 74
  improper, 23, 91
Hand-rearing, 34, 39-50, 55-62

Hand-taming, 7, 63-70
Hatching, 19, 23-7, 34-8, 83
Health guarantee, 10
Hospital cage, 28-9, 82, 87
Housing, 10-14, 54

Incubation, 19-22, 34-8

Kwik-Stop, 74, 78

Lice, 82-3
Lifespan, 7
Lutino, 15

Mating, 18-19
Millet spray, 51, 66
Mineral block, 11, 87
Mites, 15, 82-3
Molting, 15
Movement, freedom of, 10, 54, 62

Nest box, 10-11, 14-15, 18-19
Nest box inspection, 22-3
Newspaper, 11, 90
Nose, runny, 10, 78

Paint, non-toxic, 11
Pair-bonding, 18
Parsley, 91
Perches, 11-14, 22, 27, 54, 59, 82
Petamine, 11
Pied, 15
Play, 7, 14, 54, 62
Pneumonia, 78

Regurgitation, 24, 26, 42
Relationship with keeper, 7, 18, 63-71, 91
Rewarding good behavior, 7, 67, 70, 75

Sawdust, 11
Seed container, 11, 82, 90
Selecting a bird, 7-10
Sexing, 15-18
Shock, 79, 86
Sour crop, 43, 86-7
Spraddle legs, 83-6
Steam, 19
Suffocation, 38

Talking ability, 70-1
Taming, 7, 10, 63-70
Temperature, 26, 34, 38-9, 59, 63, 78-9, 82, 87
Training, 7, 27, 63-71, 91
Treats, 11, 67, 70, 75
Toys, 7, 14, 54, 73, 82, 90

Unconsciousness, 79

Vitamins, 11, 27, 42, 75
Vocalizations, 7, 18-19, 42, 46, 54-5, 58-9, 70-1

Water, 11, 19, 42, 62, 70, 78, 90
Water container, 11, 26-7, 90
Weaning, 26, 34-5, 50-4, 59-62
Wing clipping, 62, 70, 73-4, 79